O9-BTN-162

the me I **want** to be
participant's guide

Resources by John Ortberg

An Ordinary Day with Jesus
(curriculum series, with Ruth Haley Barton)

Everybody's Normal Till You Get to Know Them
(book, audio)

God Is Closer Than You Think
(book, audio, curriculum with Stephen and Amanda Sorenson)

If You Want to Walk on Water, You've Got to Get Out of the Boat
(book, audio, curriculum with Stephen and Amanda Sorenson)

Know Doubt
(book, formerly entitled *Faith and Doubt*)

The Life You've Always Wanted
(book, audio, curriculum with Stephen and Amanda Sorenson)

Living the God Life

Love Beyond Reason

Old Testament Challenge
(curriculum series, with Kevin and Sherry Harney)

When the Game Is Over, It All Goes Back in the Box
(book, audio, curriculum with Stephen and Amanda Sorenson)

the me I **want** to be
participant's guide
» becoming God's best version of you

five sessions

john ortberg
with scott rubin

ZONDERVAN®

ZONDERVAN.com/
AUTHORTRACKER
follow your favorite authors

ZONDERVAN

The Me I Want to Be Participant's Guide
Copyright © 2010 by John Ortberg

Requests for information should be addressed to:

Zondervan, *Grand Rapids, Michigan 49530*

ISBN 978-0-310-32079-1

All Scripture quotations, unless otherwise indicated, are taken from the Holy Bible, *Today's New International Version®. TNIV®.* Copyright © 2001, 2005 by Biblica, Inc.™ Used by permission of Zondervan. All rights reserved worldwide.

Scripture quotations marked NLT are taken from the *Holy Bible, New Living Translation*, copyright © 1996, 2004. Used by permission of Tyndale House Publishers, Inc., Wheaton, Illinois. All rights reserved.

Scripture quotations marked MSG are taken from *The Message.* Copyright © 1993, 1994, 1995, 1996, 2000, 2001, 2002. Used by permission of NavPress Publishing Group.

Scripture quotations marked NASB are taken from the *New American Standard Bible.* Copyright © 1960, 1962, 1963, 1968, 1971, 1972, 1973, 1975, 1977, 1995 by The Lockman Foundation. Used by permission.

Any Internet addresses (websites, blogs, etc.) and telephone numbers printed in this book are offered as a resource. They are not intended in any way to be or imply an endorsement by Zondervan, nor does Zondervan vouch for the content of these sites and numbers for the life of this book.

All rights reserved. No part of this publication may be reproduced, stored in a retrieval system, or transmitted in any form or by any means — electronic, mechanical, photocopy, recording, or any other — except for brief quotations in printed reviews, without the prior permission of the publisher.

Cover and interior design: Lindsay Lang Sherbondy with Heartland Community Church
Interior design management: Ben Fetterley

Printed in the United States of America

13 14 15 16 17 • 22 21 20 19 18 17 16 15 14 13 12 11 10 9

contents

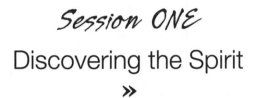

Session ONE
Discovering the Spirit

»

Discovering the Spirit

Your flourishing is never just about you. It is a "so that" kind of condition. God designed you to flourish "so that" you could be part of his redemptive project in ways that you otherwise could not. He wants you to flourish "so that" people can be encouraged, gardens can be planted, music can be written, sick people can be helped, or companies can thrive in ways they otherwise would not. When you fail to become the person God designed, all the rest of us miss out on the gift you were made to give.

The Me I Want to Be, ch. 2

» DVD Teaching Notes

As you watch the session one video teaching segment, featuring John Ortberg, take notes below on anything that stands out to you. An outline has been provided to help you follow along.

Flourishing means becoming "you-ier" — restored, not exchanged; living up to your full potential!

"Counterfeit" versions of me that I sometimes choose:

The "me" I pretend to be	I try to convince people I am important while secretly fearing I am not.
The "me" I think I should be	I have a need to try to be someone I'm not, often motivated by comparison.
The "me" other people want me to be	I don't feel free to be myself; I follow others' agendas.
The "me" I'm afraid God wants	I lack trust in God's love and plan; I equate spiritual maturity with trying hard to follow the Bible's rules.
The "me" that fails to be	I'm missing mental and emotional vitality, and my soul is weary.

But the best version of me is ...

The "me" I'm meant to be	I am fully alive inside ... and growing!

» DVD Group Discussion

1. Of the five versions of counterfeit "me's" noted in the chart on page 10, which one do you think you most gravitate toward? Why? What circumstances in your life affect this tendency?

2. God is highly concerned about you reaching your full potential — and he doesn't get discouraged in the process. John Ortberg says that we cannot follow God if we don't trust he really has our best interests at heart. Can you relate to this thought? Why or why not?

3. Where have you seen F.T.T. (failure to thrive) in the world? How about in your own life?

4. If someone were to ask you how your spiritual life is going, what factors would you consider in your response? How would you go about assessing yourself?

In *The Me I Want to Be*, Ortberg says that a wise man suggested answering this spiritual life assessment by responding to two questions:

- Am I growing more easily discouraged these days?
- Am I growing more easily irritated these days?

How would you answer these questions today? And from your answers, how would you gauge your spiritual life?

5. If flourishing is being full of joy, peace, and curiosity and possessing an openness to learning and a desire to lean into challenges, then the opposite — languishing — would mean lacking mental and emotional vitality and being uneasy, full of discontent, and self-focused. On a continuum, where would you place yourself between flourishing and languishing most of the time?

LANGUISHING   FLOURISHING

Have you ever thought of yourself as too young, too old, or too _____ (fill in the blank) to flourish? Is there any shift you need to make in your own perspective?

» Group Bible Exploration

1. Have you ever undertaken a home improvement or restoration project? What was the end result? (Very briefly share your responses.)

In restoring or fixing something, we can experience its full effectiveness and its full magnificence.

Read together 2 Corinthians 5:17:

> Therefore, if anyone is in Christ, the new creation has come: The old has gone, the new is here!

Becoming a new creation doesn't mean becoming completely different but, as Ortberg explains, being "restored to [our] intended beauty." What holds you back from leaning into becoming all God intended you to be? How does your hesitation in that area affect those around you?

2. Read together Psalm 92:12–13:

> The righteous will flourish like a palm tree, they will grow like a cedar of Lebanon; planted in the house of the LORD, they will flourish in the courts of our God.

God is interested in your *individual* restoration and growth. If you were an acorn, God would not want or expect you to become a rosebush ... he designed acorns to become oak trees. Flourishing is becoming more of what God made you to be.

Is there something you're trying to be that God did *not* design you for? Have you given up (consciously or not) on some God-given dreams? What experiences, thoughts, or reasons have contributed to that?

3. Joy is a gift that God gives us when we are flourishing ... and in step with the Holy Spirit. Read together 1 Peter 1:8:

> Though you have not seen him [Jesus], you love him ... and are filled with an inexpressible and glorious joy.

Have you ever experienced this kind of "inexpressible and glorious joy" that Peter describes? How would others describe your joy factor? What would be their evidence?

4. Rest is another factor in becoming who God made you to be. Rest is important enough that even God rested when he created the world. And Jesus tells us in Matthew 11:29 that he desires us to find rest. Read together his words:

> "Take my yoke upon you and learn from me, for I am gentle and humble in heart, and you will find rest for your souls."

What are some ways you receive rest, rejuvenation, and vitality from God that allow you to flourish? How would your calendar from the last few weeks or months reflect your engagement in these practices?

5. Imagine that you are wandering in the desert and desperately need water. What words would you use to describe your feelings upon finding it?

Read together Psalm 42:1:

> As the deer pants for streams of water, so my soul pants for you, my God.

Why do you think the psalmist chose this picture to illustrate his longing for God?

Tell about a time when you experienced this desperate, need-God-to-survive kind of desire. What would it take for you to experience a deep longing for God as a regular part of your life?

» In Closing

As you wrap up your group study, close in prayer. Ask God to help each member of your group to identify the "me" they sometimes struggle with ... and to take steps to flourish and become the "me" God intended. Pray for God's promptings this week to be strong in each person's life — and that they'd have the courage to follow them.

Before your next meeting, complete the "On Your Own Between Sessions" section that begins on page 18. Consider starting the next group meeting by sharing together what you learned from this individual exercise.

» On Your Own Between Sessions

Look back at the "counterfeit me" chart on page 10. On a piece of paper or in a journal, make a chart (see the example below) listing the "counterfeit me" options. During the next few days, keep that chart with you and periodically monitor your "me-ness" by checkmarking the appropriate "counterfeit me" when you notice it in different situations. Jot notes about the circumstances that might have influenced the "me" you were being. After a few days, observe any patterns that emerge.

EXAMPLE:

"Counterfeit Me" Options	How Often	Notes
The "me" I pretend to be	✓ ✓ ✓ ✓ ✓	I keep doing this when I am around one particular coworker. Why does my neighbor make me feel like I need to pretend?
The "me" I think I should be		
The "me" other people want me to be		
The "me" I'm afraid God wants	✓ ✓ ✓	I lack trust when it comes to following God's promptings.
The "me" that fails to be	✓	I am so tired — the baby woke up three times last night.

With God's help, reflect on this list and your tendencies and patterns. Do you see the gap between the counterfeit you that you sometimes choose and the you God made you to be? How often are you tempted to pretend that gap doesn't exist—that you are spiritually more mature or "in the flow of the Spirit" than you really are?

In *The Message* paraphrase of the Bible, Paul writes, "Rule-keeping does not naturally evolve into living by faith, but only perpetuates itself in more and more rule-keeping" (Galatians 3:12). Closing the gap doesn't come from following the rules ... or trying harder to be good. The gap—moving from the counterfeit you to the you that you want to be—can only be filled through God's grace, and by living in the flow of the Spirit. What would it look like if you were to give grace to yourself when you aren't flourishing and being the me you want to be?

As you reflect on this exercise, list three specific ways you can grow in battling the counterfeits and becoming the "me you were meant to be."

1.

2.

3.

» Recommended Reading

In preparation for session two, you may want to read chapters 7 – 10 of the book *The Me I Want to Be*, by John Ortberg. To review what you studied in session one, you also may want to read chapters 1 – 6.

Session TWO
Renewing My Mind

»

Renewing My Mind

Becoming the best version of yourself, then, rests on one simple directive: Think great thoughts! People who live great lives are people who habitually think great thoughts. Their thoughts incline them toward confidence, love, and joy. Trying to change your emotions by willpower without allowing the stream of your thoughts to be changed by the flow of the Spirit is like fumigating the house of the skunk smell while the skunks continue to live in your crawl space. But God can change the way we think.

The Me I Want to Be, ch. 8

» DVD Teaching Notes

As you watch the session two video teaching segment, featuring John Ortberg, take notes below on anything that stands out to you. An outline has been provided to help you follow along.

As you open yourself to the flow of the Spirit, you start to love God more and more — not because you *should*, but because you can't help it — and this changes your desires.

We must train the pattern of our thoughts to be toward God.

» DVD Group Discussion

1. To change the way we think, we must start by learning to monitor our thoughts. Two people in the same situation can have very different experiences, based on their ways of thinking (e.g., one may see something as a problem, the other may see it as an opportunity). Consider your thought life. Do you tend to be a "glass half-full" or "glass half-empty" kind of thinker? Explain you answer.

2. As we learn to monitor our thoughts, we must next set our mind — decide what we will think about. John Ortberg says that to "think great thoughts" is to have thoughts that incline us toward things such as confidence, love, and joy — things that move us toward God. Using the continuum below, assess your propensity to regularly think great thoughts:

RARELY   ALL
                      THE TIME

How can you increase your habit of great-thought-thinking?

3. To equip us to think great thoughts, we need to provide ourselves life-giving fuel. One highly effective tool in our thought life is God's Word. God loves us whether or not we read the Bible, but he has given us the gift of Scripture to help us flourish. Without feeling guilty about your response, how often do you read your Bible? What factors contribute to your answer? What's a practical, concrete action you can take to feed your mind with Scripture more regularly?

4. Freedom can mean different things to different people. What freedom do you personally treasure (e.g., to come and go as you please, no laws against practicing Christianity), and why?

What freedom do you have when it comes to your mind and thoughts?

There's a spiritual battle being waged by the Evil One against you and your thoughts. What control do you have in this battle? What is the danger—to you and those around you—if you choose to not monitor your thought life?

» Group Bible Exploration

1. Read together the following Scriptures:

So Jacob served seven years to get Rachel [as his wife], but they seemed like only a few days to him because of his love for her.

Genesis 29:20

"The kingdom of heaven is like treasure hidden in a field. When a man found it, he hid it again, and then in his joy went and sold all he had and bought that field. Again, the kingdom of heaven is like a merchant looking for fine pearls. When he found one of great value, he went away and sold everything he had and bought it."

Matthew 13:44–46

What kind of desire did Jacob, the man, and the merchant all have?

Have you ever experienced this kind of desire — or dream — for something or someone? Use single words (like *excitement* or *fear*) to tell the group what kind of feelings you had when you were in pursuit of your desire or dream.

Have you ever considered where your desire came from? Can you connect it to your passions or gifts?

2. Think back over your thought life from the past several days. What was the pattern of your thoughts in general (e.g., positive, discouraged, worried)? Did you find yourself consciously aware of the kinds of thoughts you entertained?

Read together 2 Corinthians 10:5:

We demolish arguments and every pretension that sets itself up against the knowledge of God, and we take captive every thought to make it obedient to Christ.

Is it a common practice for you to take your thoughts captive to God, as the Bible tells us to do? What makes that hard—or easy—for you to do?

3. You've heard the phrase "garbage in, garbage out." When you consider your thoughts, were there times this week that you allowed "garbage in" or consciously entertained thoughts you knew you shouldn't? Share a brief example.

Look up and read Psalm 139 in its entirety, if time permits. Otherwise, read together these summary verses:

> You have searched me, LORD, and you know me.... All the days ordained for me were written in your book before one of them came to be.... Search me, God, and know my heart; test me and know my anxious thoughts. (vv. 1, 16b, 23)

If God already knows the psalmist's thoughts, why does he ask God to test them?

What is the benefit in bringing our "offensive ways" (see v. 24) to our awareness and to God's? What role might forgiveness play in allowing us to flourish?

4. Read together the following Scriptures:

> Those who live according to the sinful nature have their minds set on what that nature desires; but those who live in accordance with the Spirit have their minds set on what the Spirit desires. The mind controlled by the sinful nature is death, but the mind controlled by the Spirit is life and peace. The sinful mind is hostile to God; it does not submit to God's law, nor can it do so. Those controlled by the sinful nature cannot please God.
>
> Romans 8:5–8
>
> Since, then, you have been raised with Christ, set your hearts on things above, where Christ is seated at the right hand of God. Set your minds on things above, not on earthly things.
>
> Colossians 3:1–2
>
> Do not conform to the pattern of this world, but be transformed by the renewing of your mind.
>
> Romans 12:2a

What is the common theme in these passages? How would you define "set your mind"? How do you determine what to set your mind on?

What result will you experience when you are controlled by the Spirit—in what direction will your thoughts lead you? What kind of thoughts do you have if you are controlled by your sinful nature, by the "pattern of this world"?

As you reflect on these passages, what do you hear the Spirit prompting you to do in your own life?

5. In *The Me I Want to Be*, Ortberg writes:

> When we tell people they ought to do something, we can take that "ought" in two ways — the ought of obligation and the ought of opportunity. The first kind is our duty. You *ought* to pay your taxes. You *ought* to keep your dog on a leash. You *ought* to take your drivers' test. The second kind gives us life. You *ought* to take a break. You *ought* to see the world. You *ought* to taste this cake.
>
> The "ought" of Jesus' message is mainly an ought of opportunity.

> When we become aware of this, we feel guilty because our desire for God does not run deep enough — but we cannot make ourselves desire God more by telling ourselves that we should. God is so gracious and patient, wanting us to want him, that he is willing to work with this kind of honesty. That is why we are invited to "taste and see that the LORD is good."
>
> *Taste* is an experimental word. It is an invitation from a confident chef. You don't have to commit to eating the whole thing; just try a sample — *taste*. If you don't like it, you can skip the rest. But the chef is convinced that if he can get you to take one bite, you are going to want the whole enchilada.

Do you sometimes struggle with *wanting* to desire God? If so, how do you picture God and his demeanor toward you in that struggle?

Read together Psalm 34:8:

> Taste and see that the LORD is good; blessed are those who take refuge in him.

Does this verse affect your perspective on God's heart toward you? How can enjoying all that God created help you to "taste and see that the LORD is good"?

Read together James 1:17:

> Every good and perfect gift is from above, coming down from the Father of the heavenly lights, who does not change like shifting shadows.

Have you ever considered that desiring God can be receiving pleasure from the good gifts in your life? Ponder that wonderful thought for a moment.

» In Closing

Pray together as you end this session. Ask God to help each group member to be willing to look deeply at their desires and thought life and to allow him to fully search their hearts. Pray for wisdom in seeing where God is leading each person to turn their desires toward him — how he specifically wants them to set their minds on him and his ways.

Before you meet again, complete the following "On Your Own Between Sessions" section beginning on page 34. Consider starting the next session by sharing what group members learned from this individual exercise.

» On Your Own Between Sessions

Thinking great thoughts sounds captivating, but it's also a bit ambiguous. How motivated are you to do the intentional work it may take to set your mind consistently on the presence and goodness of God—to move toward him more and more in your thought life? If you are up to the challenge, do this "on your own" exercise.

1. Start by asking God to search you and reveal your blind spots (see again Psalm 139:23–24). Review the past day or two. Can you identify any habitual thought patterns that are not honoring to you or to God? For example, do you too often dwell on the negatives in your life? Do you too readily find fault with others? Do you short-change your time with God and his Word for something else? (If you are feeling brave, ask a few close friends to reflect back to you how they have experienced you lately.) Then, as a first step in thinking great thoughts, confess any non-God-honoring thought patterns you find. Note them here:

2. Next, reflect again on these words from Romans 12:2: "Let God transform you into a new person by changing the way you think" (NLT). Simply ask God to prepare you to take steps of growth. Go ahead, ask him! Write your prayer here if you'd like:

3. Philippians 4:8—"Whatever is noble, whatever is right, whatever is pure, whatever is lovely, whatever is admirable—if anything is excellent or praiseworthy—think about such things"—offers clear-cut directions on thinking great thoughts. Using these categories (e.g., noble, lovely, pure), make a list of things in your life that fit (e.g., physical blessings, something that catches your attention in nature, family, friends, circumstances, etc.).

4. Beginning right now, take a "snapshot" of your thoughts on a regular basis for the rest of the day. Maybe you can set your watch or phone to go off every couple hours. When the timer rings, consider your thought pattern at that moment. If you find you are not thinking a Philippians 4:8 kind of thought, ask God to help you exchange it for something from your list.

5. As the day winds down, try to identify the kinds of thoughts you had to battle with Philippians 4:8. Ask God to help you increase your awareness of this thought battle you are in. And for the next week, consider letting your watch or phone timer ring regularly to help remind you to think great thoughts. Finally, choose just one specific thing you will do to grow in changing the way you think. Write it here as a reminder:

» Recommended Reading

In preparation for session three, you may want to read chapters 11 – 14 of the book *The Me I Want to Be*, by John Ortberg.

Session THREE
Redeeming My Time

Redeeming My Time

We become vulnerable to temptation when we are dissatisfied with our lives. The deeper our dissatisfaction, the deeper our vulnerability, because you were made for soul satisfaction. You cannot live without it. If we do not find soul satisfaction in God, we will look for it somewhere else, but we will look for it.

The Me I Want to Be, ch. 12

» DVD Teaching Notes

As you watch the session three video teaching segment, featuring John Ortberg, take notes below on anything that stands out to you. An outline has been provided to help you follow along.

Life in the flow of the Spirit is about more than temptation avoidance; it's about staying focused on our God-given desires and living in authenticity with others.

The pattern of our sin is related to the pattern of our gifts; we must grow in self-awareness to keep in the flow of the Spirit.

» DVD Group Discussion

1. Have you ever considered the lack of self-awareness to be danger-ous? John Ortberg says, "We often don't give serious thought to our character and purity and heart, in light of the way God would view those things—we have great self-deception and self-justification." Why are self-deception and self-justification so concerning? Is it easier to see this deception in your own life, or in others' lives? How can you increase your self-awareness?

2. Our souls are meant to be satisfied by God; that's his design. Why is it important for us to keep watch over the condition of our souls? When you are experiencing soul *dis*satisfaction, what does that look like for you personally? What most helps you in keeping your soul connected to God—desiring him and resistant to temptation?

3. Ortberg says that the pattern of our sin is related to the pattern of our gifts. In *The Me I Want to Be*, John discusses Michael Mangis' list of nine common personality types and their corresponding sin patterns. Take a few minutes to read through this information (pages 41–45) and assess your personality type.

Personality Types: Their Strengths and Weaknesses*

Reformer

Strengths	• Lives with an internal standard of what is good, noble, and beautiful
	• Calls others to live better lives
Weaknesses	• Can be arrogant when unredeemed
	• Has high standards that can lead to a secret, inner sense of inadequacy
Example	The prophet Amos, who carried a plumbline to show Israel the standard God expected of society
My Notes**	

Server

Strengths	• Lives out love in action
	• Has a natural other-centeredness that makes people feel cared for
Weaknesses	• Can use "giving" to manipulate others
	• Sometimes mistakes servanthood with fear or low esteem
Example	Martha, who was busy serving while her sister Mary sat at Jesus' feet
My Notes**	

* Summarized from Michael Mangis' book *Signature Sins: Taming Our Wayward Hearts* (InterVarsity Press, 2008).
** To be used in the "On Your Own Between Sessions" section.

Achiever

Strengths
- Has a strong desire to grow
- Has the ability to accomplish things and add value in the lives and world around them

Weaknesses
- Has the temptation to be preoccupied with one's own success
- Sometimes uses other people to receive applause or approval

Example   Solomon, who sought achievement in education, finance, culture, statecraft, and the arts

My Notes**

Artist

Strengths
- Loves beauty and goodness
- Brings imagination to life, love, and faith

Weaknesses
- Finds that the need to be different can become an end in itself
- Can be tempted to give in to impulses and live an undisciplined life

Example   King David, who had strong gifts as a poet, dancer, and composer of many psalms

My Notes**

Thinker

Strengths • Is a discoverer, inventor, and lover of logic
• Holds a passion for truth — even when it is costly

Weaknesses • Having conviction of being right can lead to arrogance
• Can be tempted to withdraw from relationships and love

Example Paul, who loved to study, reason, explore, and teach

My Notes**

Loyalist

Strengths • Is faithful and dependable when the chips are down
• Loves to be part of a great team

Weaknesses • Is prone to skepticism or cynicism
• When threatened, can be pushed into isolation by fear

Example Elisha, who became Elijah's steadfast companion and protégé

My Notes**

Enthusiast

Strengths • Has high capacity for joy and emotional expression
• Has enthusiasm that is contagious

Weaknesses • Can have a need to be the center of attention
• Has a need to avoid pain that can lead to escape or addiction

Example The apostle Peter, who was the first one to leap out of the boat — even if it meant sinking

My Notes**

Commander

Strengths • Has a passion for justice and a desire to champion a great cause
• Has charisma to lead that inspires others

Weaknesses • Has a need for power that can cause others to feel used
• Sometimes relies on fear and intimidation to get one's own way

Example Nehemiah, who was moved to action — rallying followers and defying opponents — when he heard Jerusalem was in ruins

My Notes**

Peacemaker

Strengths
- Has a natural ability to listen well and give wise counsel
- Has an easy-going, low-maintenance relational style

Weaknesses
- Has a tendency to smooth things over and avoid conflict
- Is passive

Example   Abraham, who was a peacemaker with his wife, his nephew Lot, and foreign leaders — even attempting to mediate between God and Sodom and Gomorrah

My Notes**

Do you see yourself as one personality type, or a combination of two or three? Any strength taken to an extreme can become a weakness. Do you agree with the weaknesses connected to your personality type(s)?

4. Ortberg says, "Temptation promises freedom, but makes you a slave." How?

Ortberg also states, "We are not tempted by that which repulses us," unless it happens in small, almost unnoticeable steps over time. How does awareness of your personality type help you guard against temptation?

5. How important do you consider each of the following in dealing with temptation? (Ranking scale: 1 = not at all important, 3 = somewhat important, 5 = very important)

   • Having a clear picture (ahead of time) of the kind of person you want to become and why

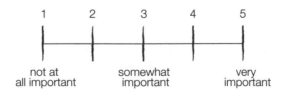

- Asking for help from another person (not being isolated from community)

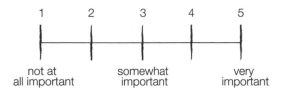

- Asking yourself, "Where will this thought/decision lead me?"

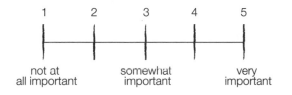

- Monitoring your soul satisfaction, on an ongoing basis, so sin doesn't look good

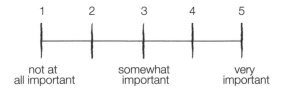

- Moving toward God when you do sin

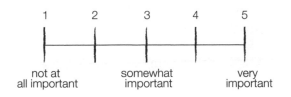

Which one or two of these actions would be most helpful to you at this point in your life?

6. When you do sin (because it happens to all of us), how easy is it for you to receive forgiveness from the Spirit? Why does it matter that you receive forgiveness? What can happen to your soul if you carry around a burden for which you've not been forgiven?

» Group Bible Exploration

1. Read together James 4:7 – 10:

> So let God work his will in you. Yell a loud no to the Devil and watch him scamper. Say a quiet yes to God and he'll be there in no time. Quit dabbling in sin. Purify your inner life. Quit playing the field. Hit bottom, and cry your eyes out. The fun and games are over. Get serious, really serious. Get down on your knees before the Master; it's the only way you'll get on your feet. (MSG)

In the above Scripture, do you see a passive or assertive response in the face of temptation? Explain.

On a scale of 1 – 10 (1 = lazy/casual; 5 = depends on the temptation; 10 = extremely imperative), how seriously do you take "temptation resistance"?

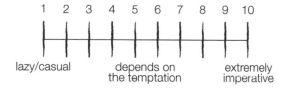

2. Read together Matthew 6:9 – 13, the "Lord's Prayer." (Even though you are probably familiar with it, try to read it with fresh eyes.)

> "This, then, is how you should pray: 'Our Father in heaven, hallowed be your name, your kingdom come, your will be done, on earth as it is in heaven. Give us today our daily bread. And forgive us our debts, as we also have forgiven our debtors. And lead us not into temptation, but deliver us from the evil one.'"

What kinds of things does Jesus include in his prayer?

When you have extended time in prayer, do you tend to include praise, worship, confession, and requests? Is there one of those that flows most readily or least readily for you? Explain.

Now read together 1 Thessalonians 5:17–18:

Pray continually, give thanks in all circumstances; for this is God's will for you in Christ Jesus.

If you were to pray the way that we are directed in this passage, would that change your prayer life? Does it seem possible, remembering that God is always present?

The Bible provides many other insights for our prayer life. On your own, you may want to look up the word *pray* in a concordance and do a Bible study on what you discover.

3. First Thessalonians 5:19 (in different versions) warns us to not *put out* (New International Version), *stifle* (New Living Translation), *suppress* (*The Message*), or *quench* (King James Version) the Holy Spirit in our lives. What makes you ignore or suppress the Holy Spirit's promptings? When are you most open to the Spirit's work in your life?

Read together the apostle Paul's words in 1 Corinthians 10:13:

> No temptation has overtaken you except what is common to us all. And God is faithful; he will not let you be tempted beyond what you can bear. But when you are tempted, he will also provide a way out so that you can endure it.

Have you ever wondered if God can truly relate to your temptations? How does this verse make you feel regarding God's understanding of your struggles?

Do you ever struggle with a sense of hope that you can grow stronger in facing the temptations in your life? How does this Scripture affect your "hope quotient"?

» In Closing

As you finish your study today, pray together, asking God to help each member of your group to grow in their ability to talk to him continually throughout the day, about everything. Pray for openness to the Holy Spirit as each person faces temptations. And ask God to give each person the courage to deal with their own pattern of sin ... to grow in awareness of and resistance toward it ... and then to continue to move toward staying in the flow of the Spirit.

Before session four, complete the "On Your Own Between Sessions" section beginning on page 54. Consider starting the next group meeting by sharing what each group member learned from this individual exercise.

» On Your Own Between Sessions

During session three's group discussion time, you discussed Michael Mangis' personality chart on pages 41–45. Find that chart again, and this time use the "My Notes" section (or the space below, or your journal) to jot down your thoughts to the following exercise.

1. Reflect on your past week. Where have you indulged in your strength's weakness (in thought, word, or action) and moved out of the flow of the Spirit? Are there any patterns to where or when this happened?

2. Is there anyone you need to seek forgiveness from, if your temptation resulted in sin?

3. Before you are tempted by your sin's pattern again, which of the following will you try?

- Having a clear picture (ahead of time) of the kind of person you want to become and why
- Asking for help from another person (not being isolated from community; seeking an accountability partner)
- Asking yourself, "Where will this thought/decision lead me?"
- Monitoring your soul satisfaction, on an ongoing basis, so sin doesn't look appealing
- Moving toward God when you do sin

After you have considered these insights, talk to God about your thoughts. Ask him to strengthen your resolve and give you courage to grow in your desire for him instead of your desire for sin. Record your prayer here if you like.

» Recommended Reading

In preparation for session four, you may want to read chapters 15 – 18 of the book *The Me I Want to Be*, by John Ortberg.

Session FOUR
Deepening My Relationships

»

Deepening My Relationships

A wise man once said that just as the three laws of real estate are "location, location, location," the three laws of relationship are "observation, observation, observation." People who give life to us are people who notice us. They know what we love and fear. When we work to truly notice someone else, love for them grows. When we work to truly observe another person, in that self-forgetfulness our own soul flourishes.

The Me I Want to Be, ch. 16

» DVD Teaching Notes

As you watch the session four video teaching segment, featuring John Ortberg, take notes below on anything that stands out to you. An outline has been provided to help you follow along.

Life-giving relationships need to be a top priority in your life.
You flourish best when connected to God and his people.

Living in isolation can easily lead to temptation or discouragement.

Connectedness brings the gifts of:
   Delight (through serving others you are blessed)

Commitment (to community)

Love (opportunities to follow the Spirit's lead)

Joy (true, deep-in-the-soul richness)

Belonging (through God's grace)

» DVD Group Discussion

1. As with "location, location, location" in real estate, if the three laws of relationship are "observation, observation, observation," what does it do to our spirit when someone truly notices or remembers something about us? Identify some loving people in your own life. How are they life-givers to you?

What can you do to increase your observation skills toward other people? How does it change your focus when you begin to observe others more deeply?

2. Depending on your feeling of connectedness with God and his people, you will land somewhere on the continuum between flourishing and languishing. Where would you currently put yourself in that range?

LANGUISHING   FLOURISHING

   What circumstances in your life tend to pull you toward flourishing? What about toward languishing?

3. Why is the commitment to community so important to our spiritual lives? Share some tangible ways you have been impacted by community. Why do you think it is so important that the church gets community right?

4. Describe one specific way you *received* the gift of love from someone this week.

Now describe one specific way you *gave* the gift of love to someone this week. Did you miss any opportunities to love? Did you notice your missed opportunity when it happened or realize it later? What was your heart's response?

5. Why is a sense of belonging something people will work so hard to find, even if it isn't through positive means (e.g., joining a gang)? Is there anyone who desires the gift of belonging from you, but you have not given it to them? What's stopping you?

» Group Bible Exploration

1. Just as a new tree or bush needs its roots fertilized and must have room in the ground to spread and grow, God says that the growth of our spiritual "roots" matters immensely.

   Look up and read together the apostle Paul's beautiful prayer in Ephesians 3:14–20, noting especially verses 17b–18 (set in italic):

   > For this reason I kneel before the Father, from whom every family in heaven and on earth derives its name. I pray that out of his glorious riches he may strengthen you with power through his Spirit in your inner being, so that Christ may dwell in your hearts through faith. *And I pray that you, being rooted and established in love, may have power, together with all the Lord's people, to grasp how wide and long and high and deep is the love of Christ,* and to know this love that surpasses knowledge—that you may be filled to the measure of all the fullness of God. Now to him who is able to do immeasurably more than all we ask or imagine, according to his power that is at work within us . . .

   What does Paul specifically instruct Christ-followers to be rooted in? What are some ways we can grow our spiritual roots?

2. Read together Hebrews 10:24–25a:

> Let us consider how we may spur one another on toward love and good deeds, not giving up meeting together, as some are in the habit of doing, but encouraging one another.

Why does a commitment to community matter to our individual spiritual health? What are the benefits of regularly being together with other believers?

In *The Me I Want to Be*, John Ortberg writes:

> Every day, everyone you know faces life with eternity on the line, and life has a way of beating people down. Every life needs a cheering section. Every life needs a shoulder to lean on once in a while. Every life needs a prayer to lift them up to God. Every life needs a hugger to wrap some arms around them sometimes. Every life needs to hear a voice saying, "Don't give up."

What adjustments, if any, do you need to make in your life to receive the gift of community — the kind of encouragement Ortberg mentions above — on a regular basis?

3. Read together the following Scriptures:

> "By this everyone will know that you are my disciples, if you love one another."
>
> John 13:35
>
> Love must be sincere. Hate what is evil; cling to what is good. Be devoted to one another in love. Honor one another above yourselves.
>
> Romans 12:9–10

Ortberg talks about giving and receiving the gift of love when you are in life-giving relationships. How can loving someone help *you* experience more love? What kind of person do you become when you love people?

First John 3:14 says anyone "who does not love abides in death" (NASB). If you choose to be unloving, what is your attitude likely to be toward temptation or being in the flow of the Spirit?

4. The Bible has a lot to say about joy. And Ortberg says that being connected in relationship brings the gift of joy. Do you think joy differs from happiness? If so, how?

Read the following Scriptures:

... the joy of the LORD is your strength.

Nehemiah 8:10

Satisfy us in the morning with your unfailing love, that we may sing for joy and be glad all our days.

Psalm 90:14

A cheerful look brings joy to the heart, and good news makes for good health.

Proverbs 15:30, NLT

So the women hurried away from [Jesus'] tomb, afraid yet filled with joy, and ran to tell his disciples.

Matthew 28:8

Why does joy matter in our lives, according to the verses you just read?

5. Regarding the gift of belonging we can receive through community, Ortberg shares his daughter's metaphor of the dock (symbolizing family/home/belonging) and the boat (symbolizing personal independence) ... and that we all were given some kind of "launching" from our family of origin. Describe your growing-up experience as it relates to your sense of belonging. Were you content on the dock or always trying to get in the boat? Were you unsure where your dock was, or never given a boat?

Read together 1 Peter 2:9:

> But you are a chosen people, a royal priesthood, a holy nation, God's special possession, that you may declare the praises of him who called you out of darkness into his wonderful light.

According to this verse, to whom do we belong? Why does belonging matter to our spiritual growth?

» In Closing

As you close this session, pray together, asking God to help each group member not only *seek* life-giving relationships but *provide* them to others. Ask God to help each person receive the gifts of Delight, Commitment, Love, Joy, and Belonging through God-honoring relationships.

And, if there are places where group members are not receiving the gifts that come from connectedness, ask God to give opportunities for new relationships and growth.

Before session five, complete the "On Your Own Between Sessions" section beginning on page 70. Consider starting the next meeting by having group members share what they learned from this individual exercise.

»On Your Own Between Sessions

John Ortberg writes in *The Me I Want to Be*, "When you are loved, it is not just that you receive more from someone else, but also that you become more yourself. You-ier. Love brings the power to become the me I want to be. Loving people are literally life-givers. That is connectedness."

Because you are made in God's image, you were designed to be in relationship with others. It's in relationships where you can flourish and become more of the me you want to be! This coming week, evaluate your connectedness to life-giving relationships. As a first step, answer the questions below in the Connectedness Inventory (from *The Me I Want to Be* book).

Yes	No	When something goes wrong, do I have at least one friend I can easily talk with about it?
Yes	No	Do I have a friend I can drop in on at any time without calling ahead?
Yes	No	Is there someone who could accurately name my biggest fears and temptations?
Yes	No	Do I have one or more friends whom I meet with regularly?
Yes	No	Do I have a friend I know well enough to trust their confidentiality?
Yes	No	If I received good news like a promotion, do I have a friend I would call immediately just to let them know?

Reflect on this exercise and the past session's discussion with your small group. Then respond to the following questions and thoughts.

Who knows you well? Do you have current relationships that have potential to become life-giving relationships where you are fully known? Take some time right now to talk to God about those current and potential relationships. Is there something God is asking you to do with one of those friendships ... perhaps schedule a time to get coffee or to share something on your heart?

You can be loved best when you are fully known—willing to take off the mask and share your heart. To be fully known takes courage. James 5:16 says, "Confess your sins to each other and pray for each other so that you may be healed." Sharing and confessing your sin with a trusted friend can be difficult, but also freeing ... and healing. Do you have someone in your life with whom you can experience deep sharing, and even confession and healing?

Finally, how would you evaluate the degree to which you are receiving the gifts of connectedness? In the blank after each word, enter 1 (often), 2 (sometimes), or 3 (rarely).

Delight = _____

Commitment = _____

Love = _____

Joy = _____

Belonging = _____

If you gave yourself mostly 1s and 2s, congratulations on your relational investment! But, if you answered mostly 2s and 3s, don't give up! Ask God to reveal areas where you need to grow in relationship-building and to help you experience his gifts through existing and new friendships.

Close your reflection time with a prayer of thanksgiving for God's gifts—those you have right now, as well as those he has in store for you!

» Recommended Reading

In preparation for session five, you may want to read chapters 19–22 of the book *The Me I Want to Be*, by John Ortberg.

Session FIVE

Transforming My Experience

»

Transforming My Experience

There can be no learning without novelty. There can be no novelty without risk. We cannot grow unless there has been a challenge to what is familiar and comfortable. The Spirit leads us into adventure. The Spirit leads us into a dangerous world. To ask for the Spirit is to ask for risk.

The Me I Want to Be, ch. 22

» DVD Teaching Notes

As you watch the session five video teaching segment, featuring John Ortberg, take notes below on anything that stands out to you. An outline has been provided to help you follow along.

Every problem is an invitation to grow in the flow of the Spirit.

Ask for a mountain.

You will know *your* mountain because it will tap into your greatest strengths and deepest passions.

»DVD Group Discussion

1. John Ortberg says that we sometimes yearn for a problem-free life, but such an existence would actually be death by boredom. Do you believe that? Do you tend to look at challenges as positive or negative things?

What are some of the challenges you faced this past week, and what was your typical response to them (e.g., energetic, irritated, patient)? Why?

This is how u grow old – allow every-thing to fall off around u until all that we see is love

"granny"
Brandt.

2. In the story of Granny Brand, we heard of a woman who embodied the statement, "Life is not about comfort." If it's true that we learn and grow best when our comfort is challenged, how does this affect your perspective on a situation you are currently facing? What might help you respond with an attitude that's more in the flow of the Spirit? What kind of emotions stir in you when you think about the fact that God wants to use you to tackle a specific "mountain"?

3. Think of a time when you faced a challenge that made you focus on the needs of others instead of your own. Describe that experience to the group. Do you think you flourish more when you are focusing on your own needs or the needs of others, and why?

4. How do you tend to view becoming the person God made you to be?

- A single pursuit woven throughout your daily life
- One of many pursuits in your life
- Other _____

Explain your answer.

»Group Bible Exploration

1. God calls each of us to live for something more than ourselves. Read together the words of Jesus in Mark 8:34:

> "Whoever wants to be my disciple must deny themselves and take up their cross and follow me."

When Jesus invited his followers to "take up their cross," do you think they understood that it was a call to sacrificial love and serving? When you hear these words, do you tend to think about it as a burden or opportunity ... or both? Why?

2. Read Numbers 13:26–33, the account of the Israelites' report on exploring the land of Canaan. Here are the key verses:

> They gave Moses this account: "We went into the land to which you sent us, and it does flow with milk and honey.... But the people who live there are powerful, and the cities are fortified and very large.... Then Caleb ... said, "We should go up and take possession of the land, for we can certainly do it." But the men who had gone up with him said, "We can't attack those people; they are stronger than we are.... We seemed like grasshoppers in our own eyes, and we looked the same to them." (vv. 27, 28, 30–31, 33b)

How did most of the men respond to the challenges that faced them? How did Caleb respond? What do you think allowed Caleb to have a different perspective? Do you think you would have responded the way Caleb did ... or the way the others did? Why?

Whether you are fearful or fearless, take to heart John Ortberg's words:

> The Spirit wants to make you a dangerous person. The Spirit wants to make you threatening to all the forces of injustice and apathy and complacency that keep our world from flourishing. The Spirit wants to make you dangerously noncompliant in a broken world.

3. Read together Joshua 14:10 – 12, Caleb's testimony four-plus decades later:

> "Now then, just as the LORD promised, he has kept me alive for forty-five years ... while Israel moved about in the wilderness. So here I am today, eighty-five years old! I am still as strong today as the day Moses sent me out; I'm just as vigorous to go out to battle now as I was then. Now give me this hill country that the LORD promised me that day. You yourself heard then that the Anakites were there and their cities were large and fortified, but, the LORD helping me, I will drive them out just as he said."

Years after first exploring the Promised Land, Caleb's hunger for following God in the midst of challenge was still there! Reflect a moment on your own life. Over the years, do you feel that you have grown more open to the adventures God is calling you to ... or more often miss those promptings? Why?

Do you think it matters that Caleb was focusing on a cause bigger than himself? If so, do you need to do any life "rearranging" to help you focus on a cause bigger than yourself?

4. We often tend to think that each person who faces the challenge—the mountain—God is calling them to feels completely confident in their ability. Read this statement of the apostle Paul in 1 Corinthians 2:3–5:

> I came to you in weakness — timid and trembling. And my message and my preaching were very plain. Rather than using clever and persuasive speeches, I relied only on the power of the Holy Spirit. I did this so you would trust not in human wisdom but in the power of God. (NLT)

What did Paul rely on to carry out what God had called him to do?

Now read Paul's words in Romans 12:6−8:

> In his grace, God has given us different gifts for doing certain things well. So if God has given you the ability to prophesy, speak out with as much faith as God has given you. If your gift is serving others, serve them well. If you are a teacher, teach well. If your gift is to encourage others, be encouraging. If it is giving, give generously. If God has given you leadership ability, take the responsibility seriously. And if you have a gift for showing kindness to others, do it gladly. (NLT)

Which gift or ability is each person called to use in facing the mountain God has called them to? What happens if each person doesn't choose to use their individual gift? On the other hand, what could happen if everyone did?

In *The Me I Want to Be*, Ortberg writes:

> How will you recognize your mountain? There is no formula. Just as in every other area of your growth, your mountain will not look exactly like anyone else's. But often you will recognize it because it lies at the intersection of the tasks that tap into your greatest strengths and the needs that tap into your deepest passions. Yet know this for sure: *God has a mountain with your name on it.*

Dream for a moment about what your mountain could be. Do you believe, really, that there's one with *your* name on it? If you are open to it, share your thoughts with the group.

» In Closing

As you wrap up this final session, close in prayer. Ask God to help each group member see the challenges in their lives as opportunities for the Spirit to be at work ... and that he would give each person courage to find their mountain and take a risk for his kingdom. Help celebrate what God has done in each person through the conversations in this DVD study.

Then, continue to pursue God's activity in your life by completing the "On Your Own in the Coming Days" section beginning on page 85.

» On Your Own in the Coming Days

It's easy to talk about and even desire to be the person God made you to be. To put that into action means putting that pursuit above all else. The exercise below will require your heart to be open to God's call on your life to make a difference. Are you ready?

Carve out some time to explore these questions and activities:

1. Consider the mountain — the challenge — that God has for you. Have you ever asked God for a mountain ... your mountain? If not, what keeps you from making this request? If fear, uncertainty, or another reason enters your mind, invite God to replace that reason with trust and courage.

2. Next, write out some of your deepest passions, gifts, and desires. Do you see any connections or patterns? If you feel stuck, ask a close friend or family member to help you recognize these in your life.

3. Now explore your "world." Is God at work in any arenas in your life where you might be able to use your strengths? In prayer, ask him to open a door, to show you the mountain/challenge he has for you. And when he gives you your mountain, go climb it!

Remember these words from John Ortberg:

> Don't ask for comfort. Don't ask for ease. Don't ask for manageable. Ask to be given a burden for a challenge bigger than yourself, that can make a difference in the world, that will require the best you have to give it and then leave some space for God besides. Ask for a task that will keep you learning and growing and uncomfortable and hungry.

The Me I Want to Be

Becoming God's Best Version of You

John Ortberg

In *The Me I Want to Be*, John Ortberg—the bestselling author of *When the Game Is Over, It All Goes Back in the Box*; *God Is Closer Than You Think*; and *The Life You've Always Wanted*—helps you gauge your spiritual health and measure the gap between where you are now and where God intends you to be. Then he provides detailed tasks and exercises to help you live in the flow of the Spirit, circumventing real-world barriers—pain and sorrow, temptations, self-doubt, sin—to flourish even in a dark and broken world.

As you start living in the flow, you will feel:

—a deeper connection with God
—a growing sense of joy
—an honest recognition of your brokenness
—less fear, more trust
—a growing sense of being "rooted in love"
—a deeper sense of purpose

God invites you to join him in crafting an abundant and joy-filled life. *The Me I Want to Be* shows you how to graciously accept his invitation.

Hardcover, Jacketed: 978-0-310-27592-3

Pick up a copy at your favorite bookstore or online!

The Me I Want to Be Curriculum Kit

Becoming God's Best Version of You

John Ortberg

The Me I Want to Be church-wide book and video-based experience is a powerful operator's manual to help you and your group learn how God's perfect vision for your life is not just that you are saved by grace, but that you must also live by grace, flourishing with the Spirit flowing through you. Join author and pastor John Ortberg as he guides your group toward true spiritual growth.

The Me I Want to Be curriculum kit includes a "Getting Started" guide, a participant's guide, a five-session DVD, and a hardcover edition of the book, *The Me I Want to Be*.

Curriculum Kit: 978-0-310-32081-4

Pick up a copy at your favorite bookstore or online!

monvee®

THE FUTURE
OF SPIRITUAL
FORMATION

Monvee is a revolutionary tool designed to handcraft spiritual growth plans. Based on your unique characteristics, Monvee will craft a growth plan that fits how you're made, how you learn, and even your stage in life.

Using revolutionary assessment technology, the Monvee discovery process takes into consideration thirty-four different aspects of an individual. Then, it sorts through thousands of resources, practices, audio and video messages to create a tailor-made plan. The plans are never too much to handle, and Monvee gives multiple options so each area of a plan can be changed to more perfectly suit each user.

TO FIND OUT MORE ABOUT MONVEE VISIT
WWW.MONVEE.COM

Share Your Thoughts

With the Author: Your comments will be forwarded to the author when you send them to *zauthor@zondervan.com*.

With Zondervan: Submit your review of this book by writing to *zreview@zondervan.com*.

Free Online Resources at
www.zondervan.com

Zondervan AuthorTracker: Be notified whenever your favorite authors publish new books, go on tour, or post an update about what's happening in their lives at www.zondervan.com/authortracker.

Daily Bible Verses and Devotions: Enrich your life with daily Bible verses or devotions that help you start every morning focused on God. Visit www.zondervan.com/newsletters.

Free Email Publications: Sign up for newsletters on Christian living, academic resources, church ministry, fiction, children's resources, and more. Visit www.zondervan.com/newsletters.

Zondervan Bible Search: Find and compare Bible passages in a variety of translations at www.zondervanbiblesearch.com.

Other Benefits: Register yourself to receive online benefits like coupons and special offers, or to participate in research.

ZONDERVAN®

ZONDERVAN.com/
AUTHORTRACKER
follow your favorite authors